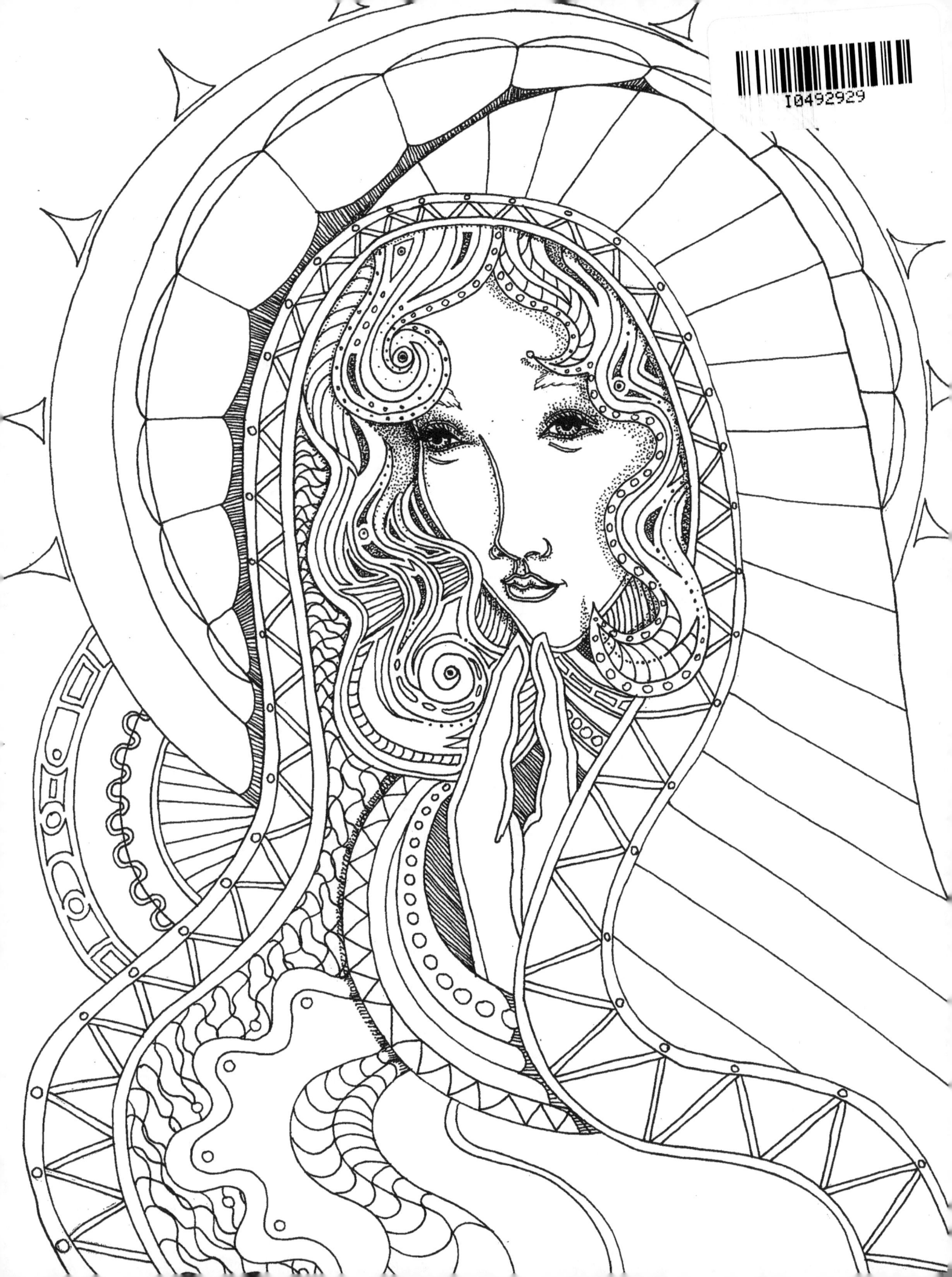
I0492929

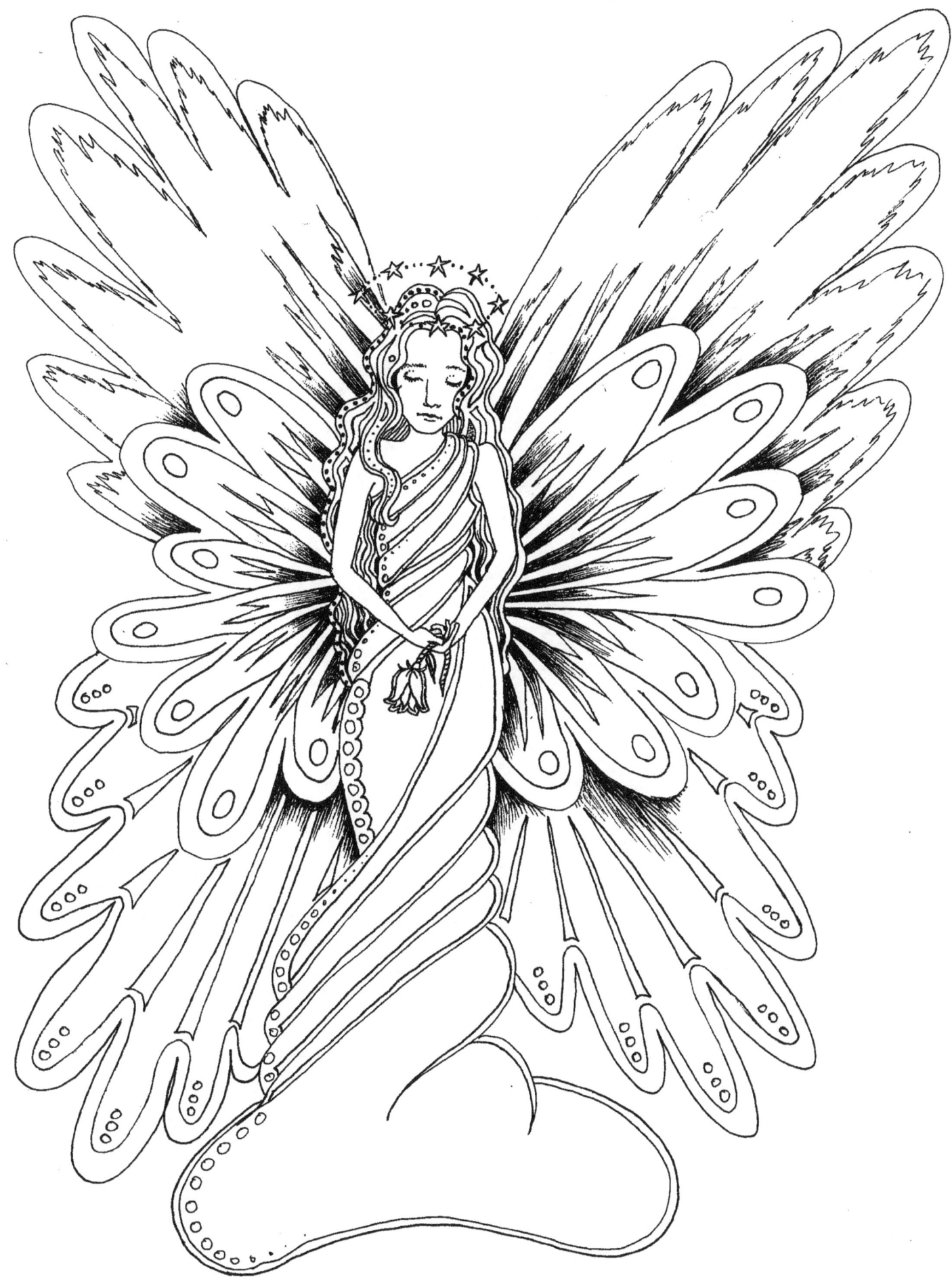

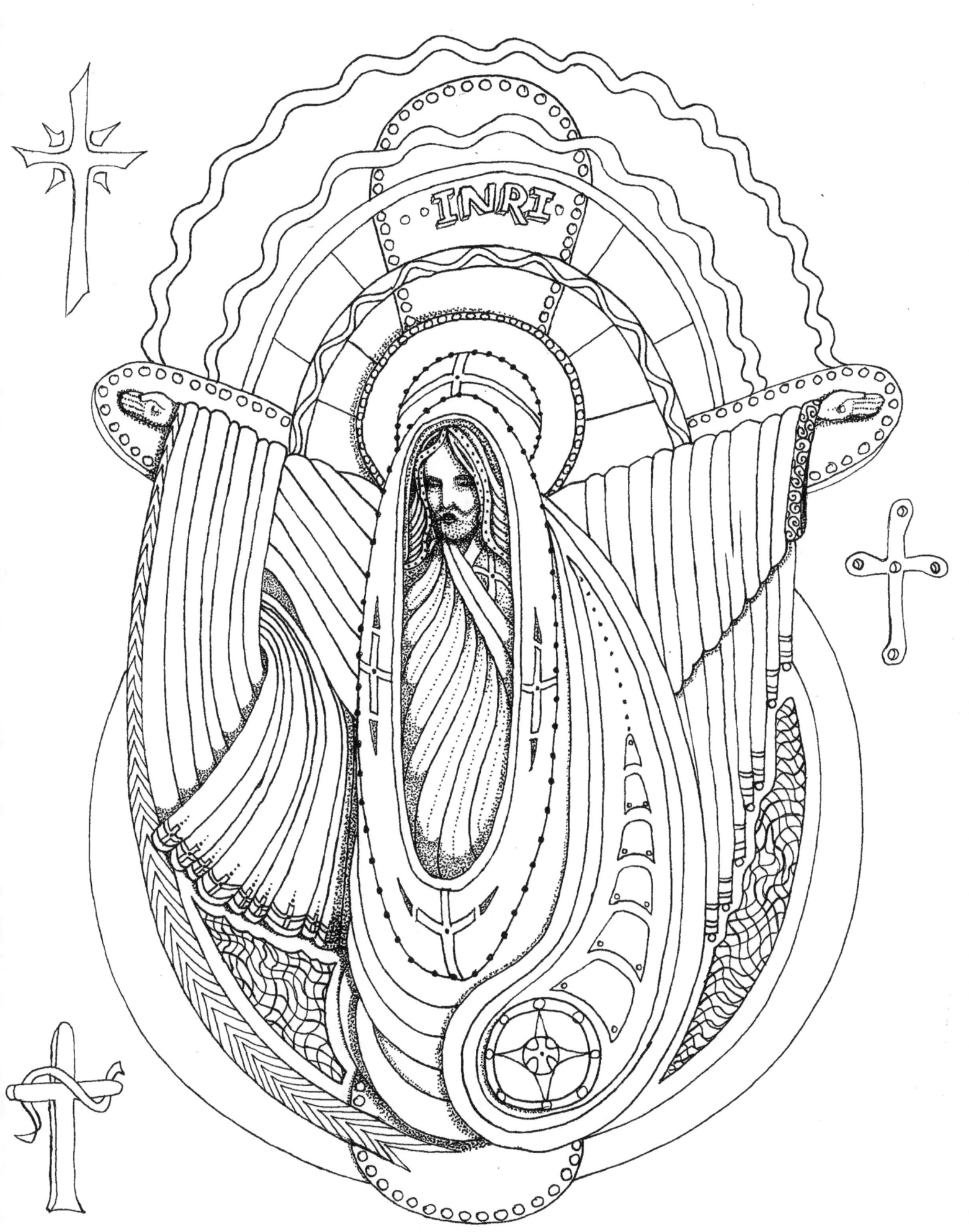

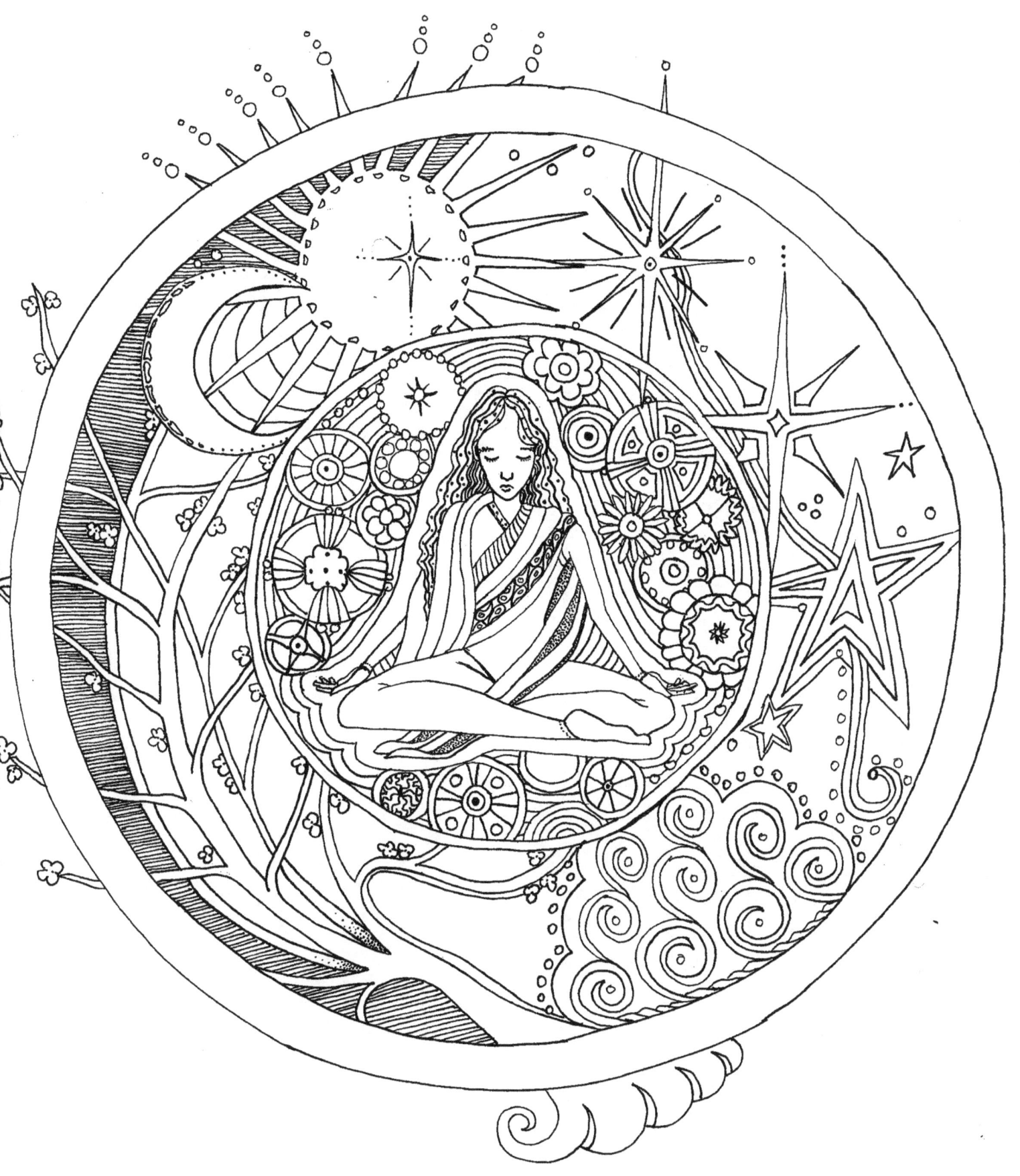

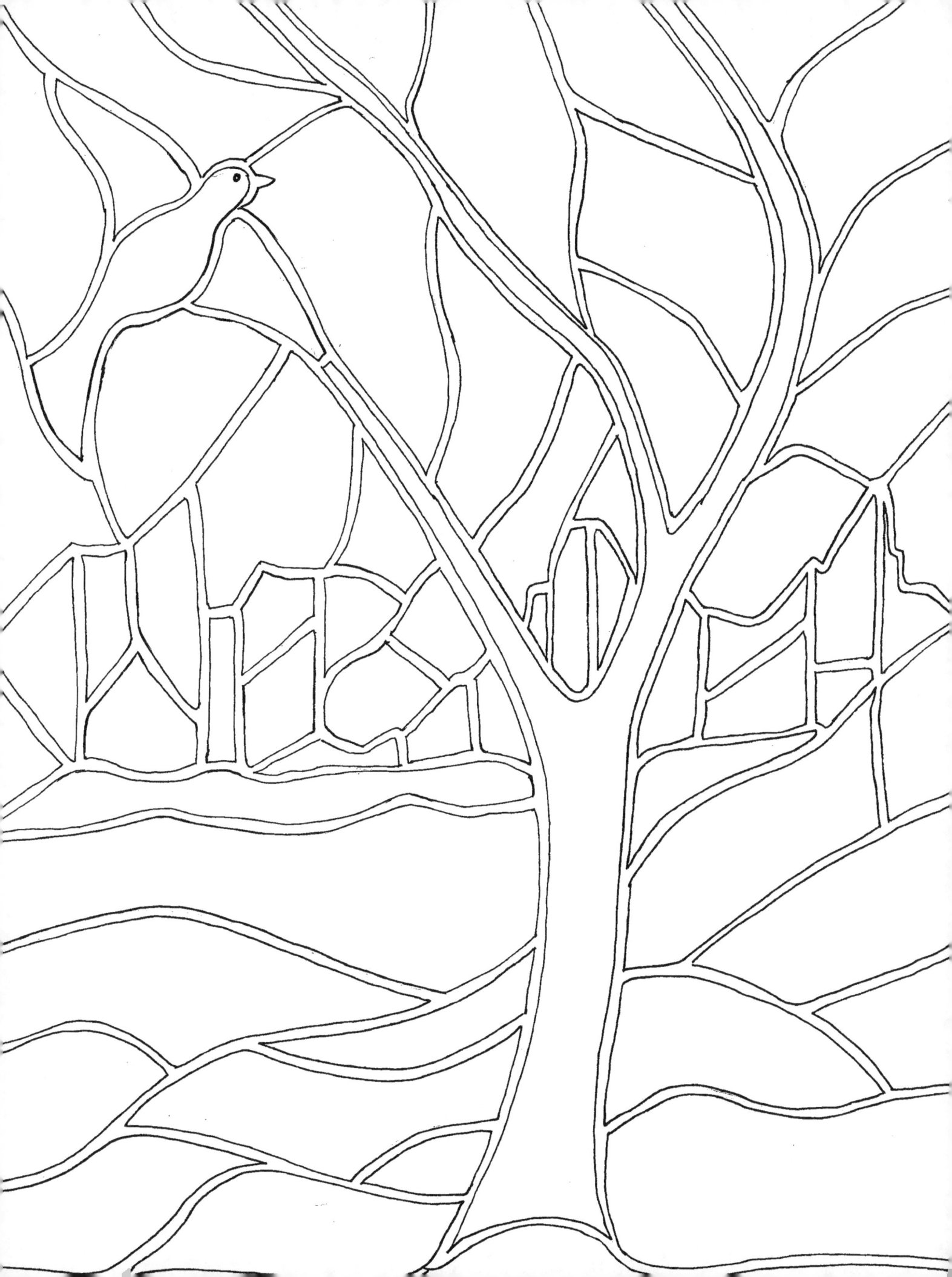

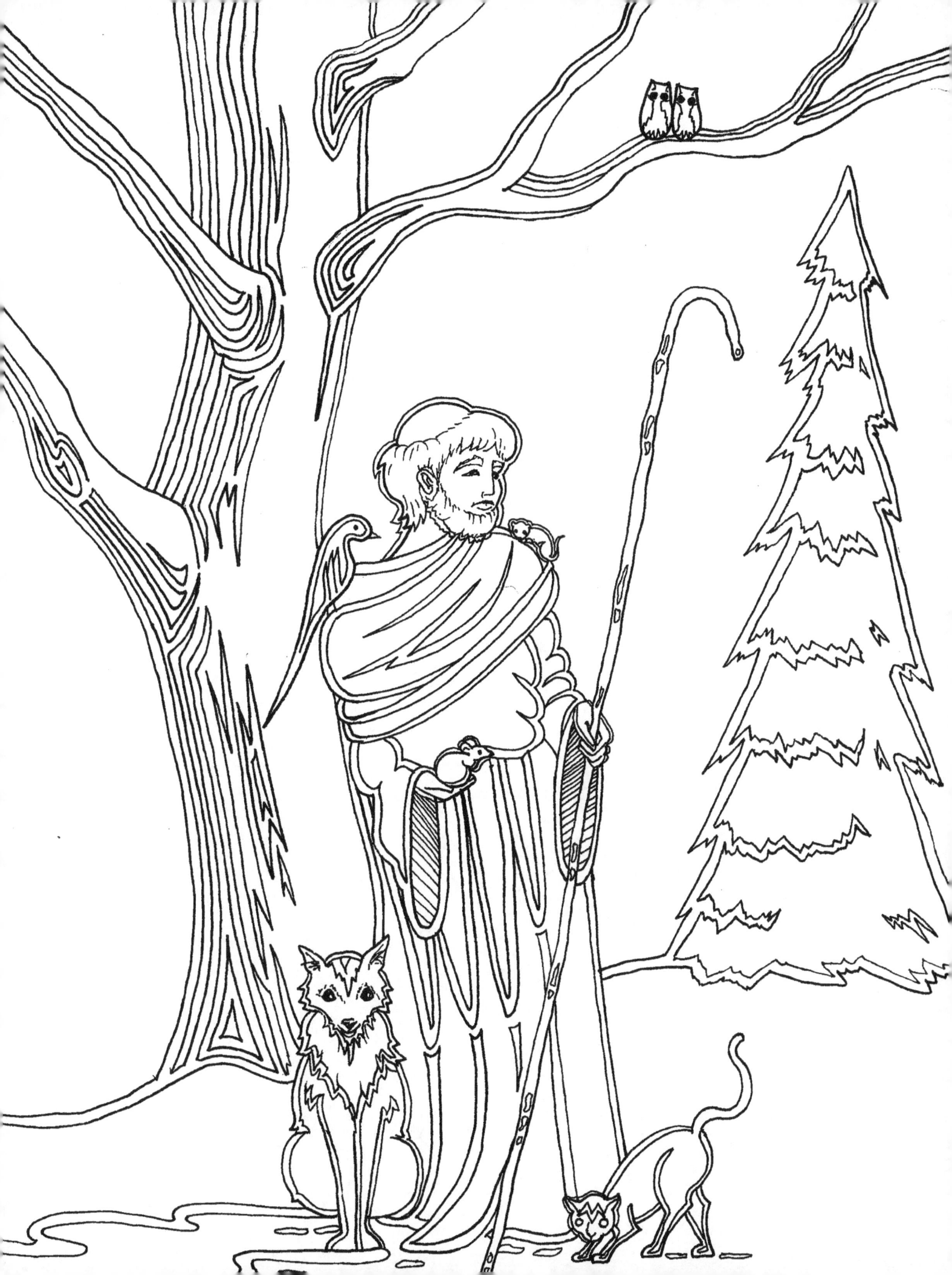

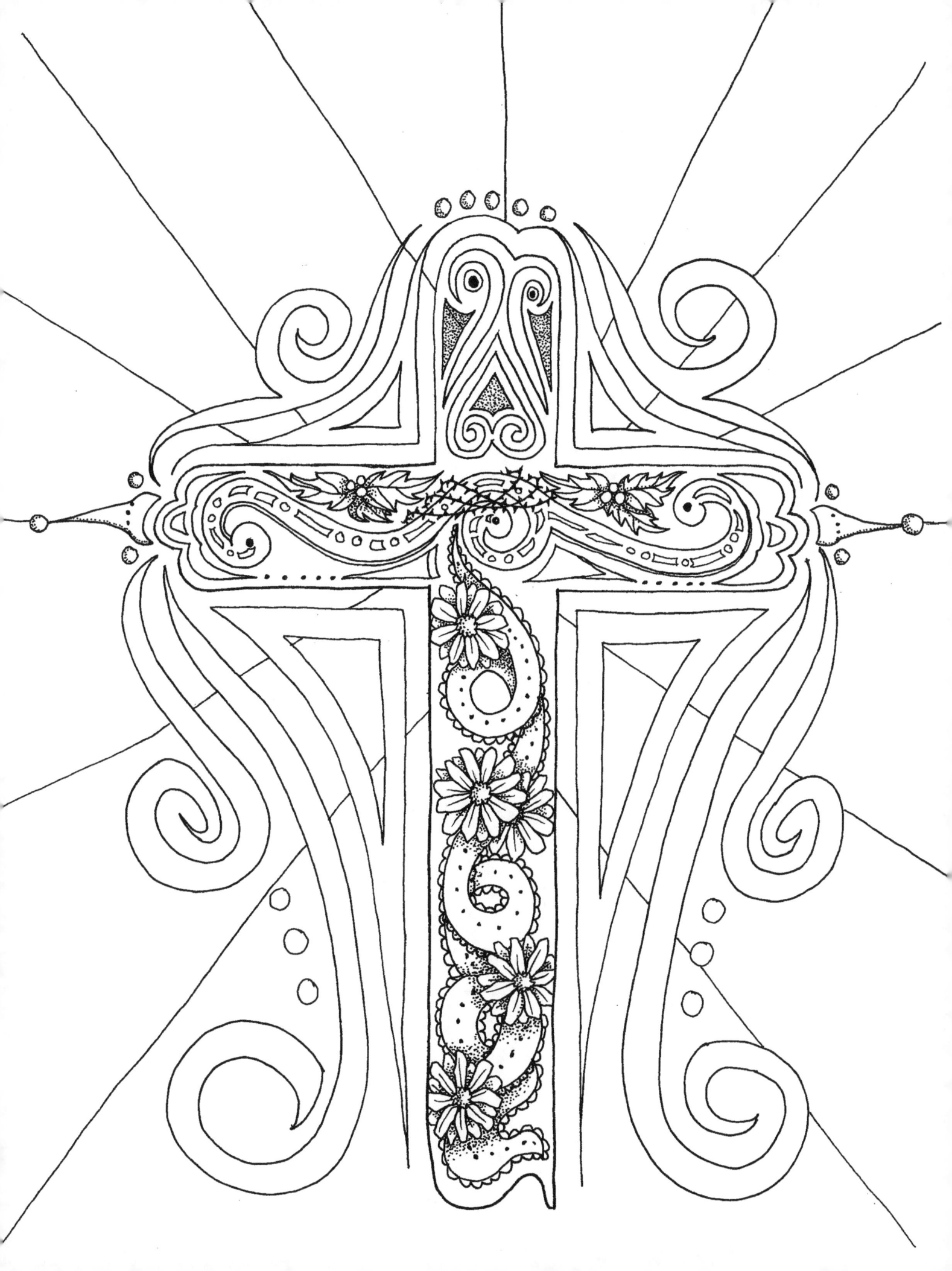

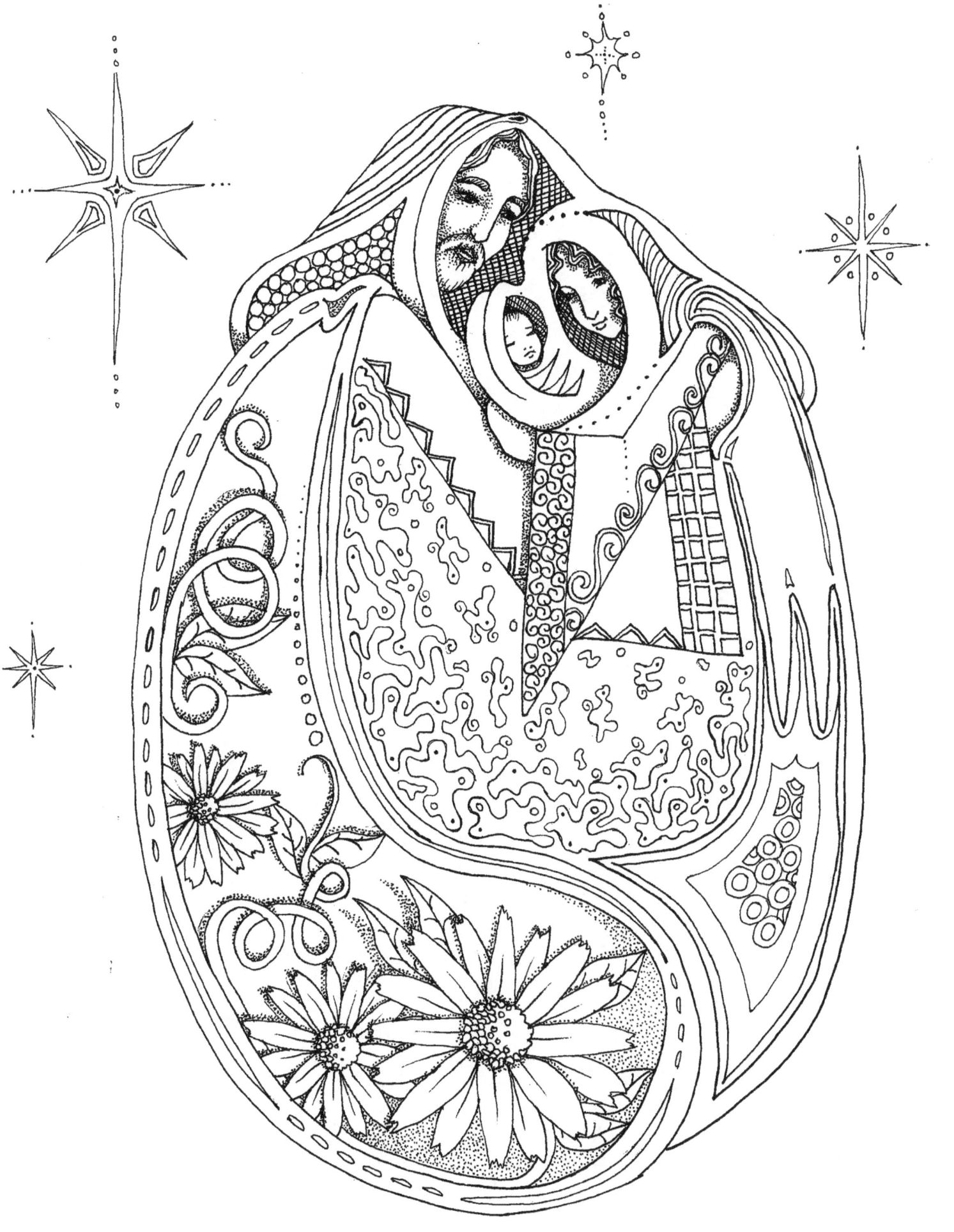

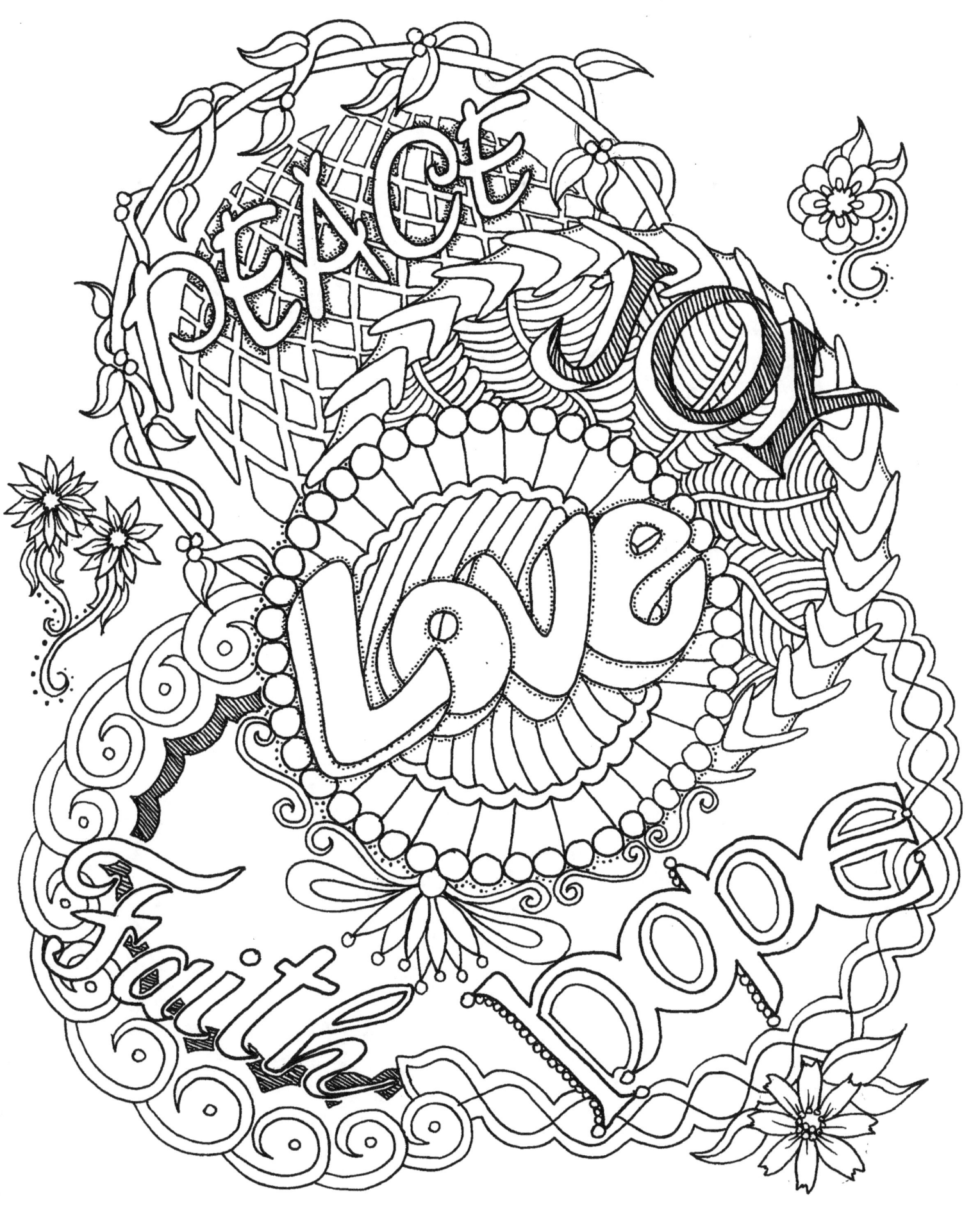

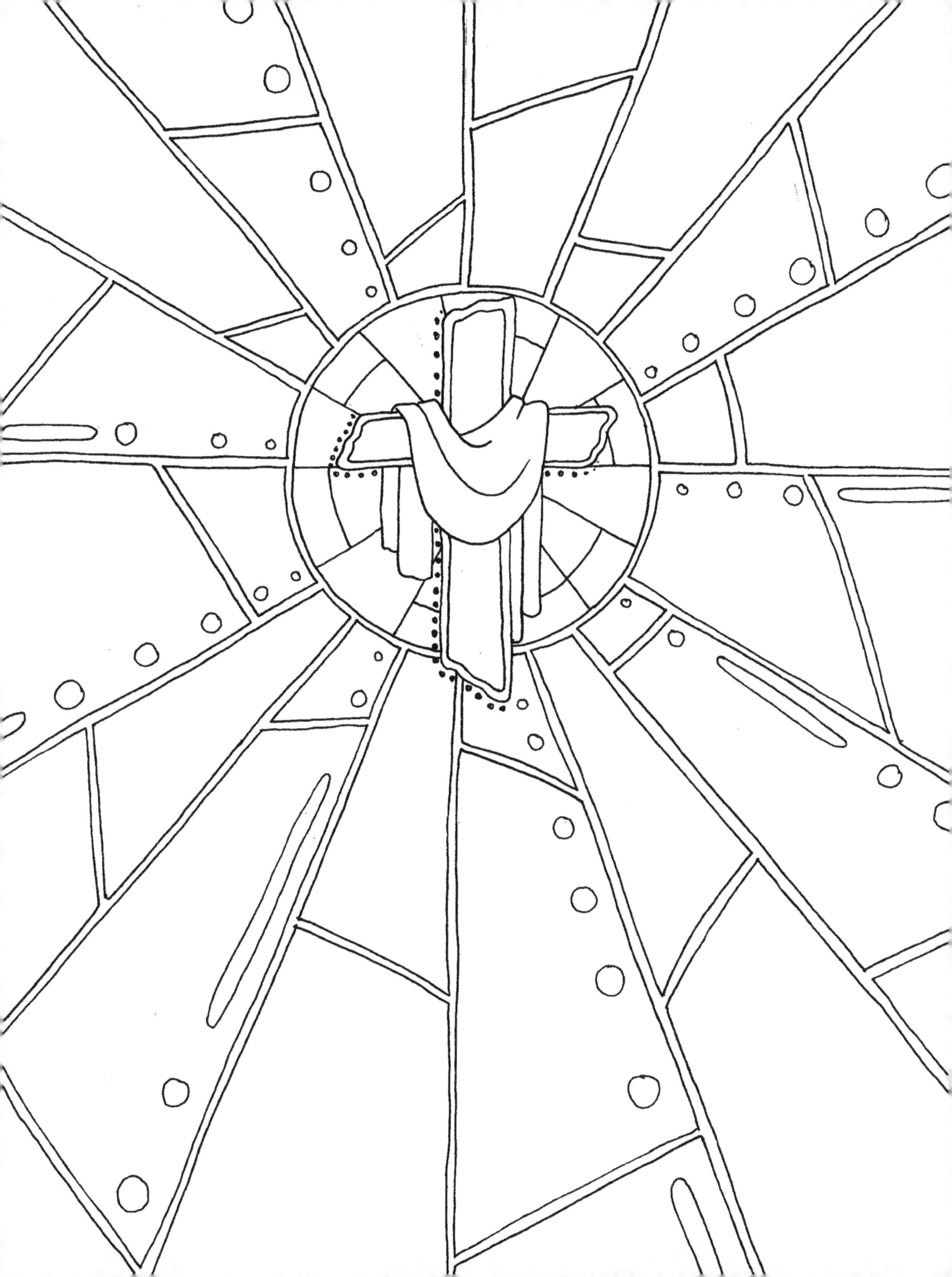

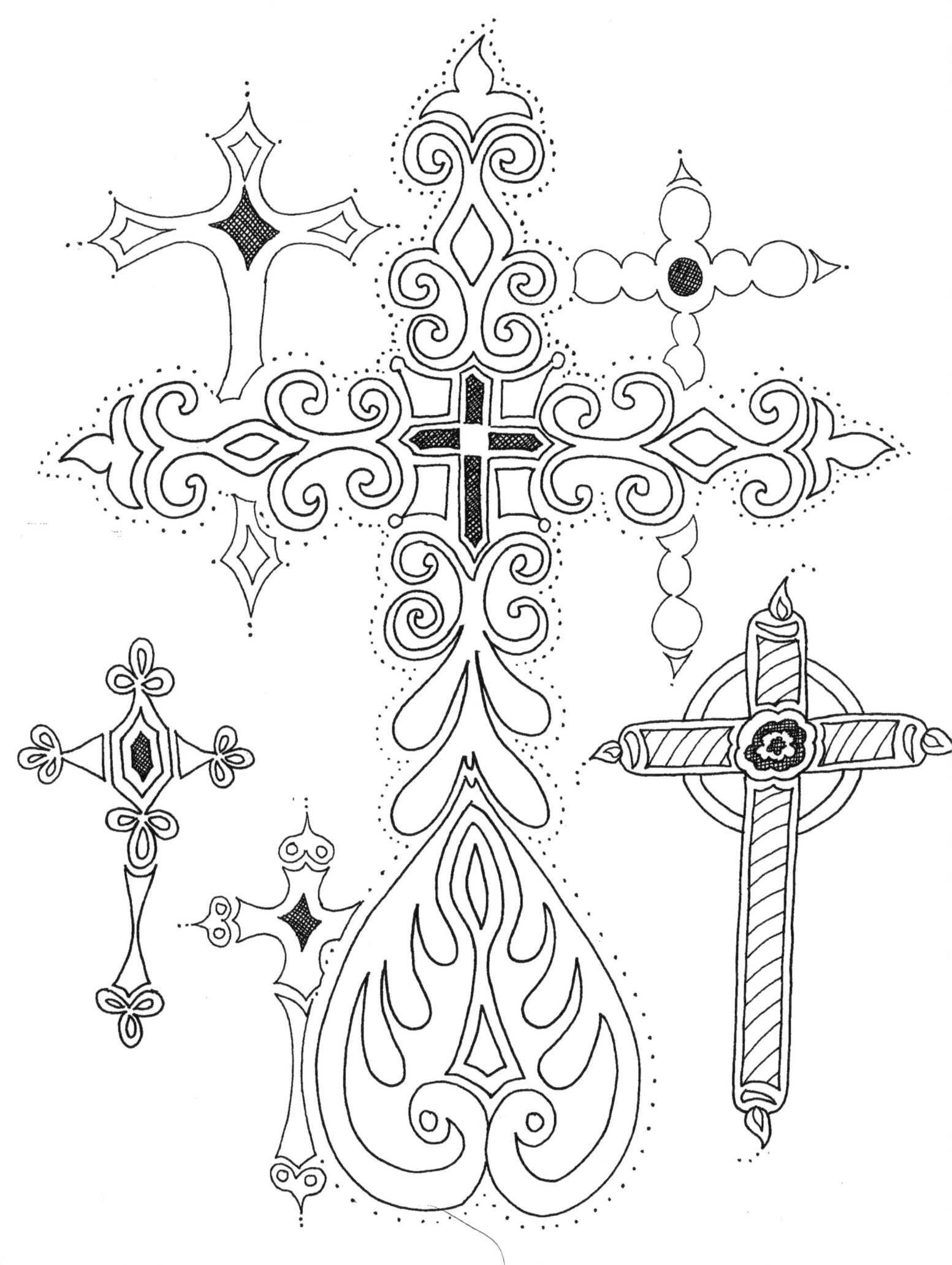

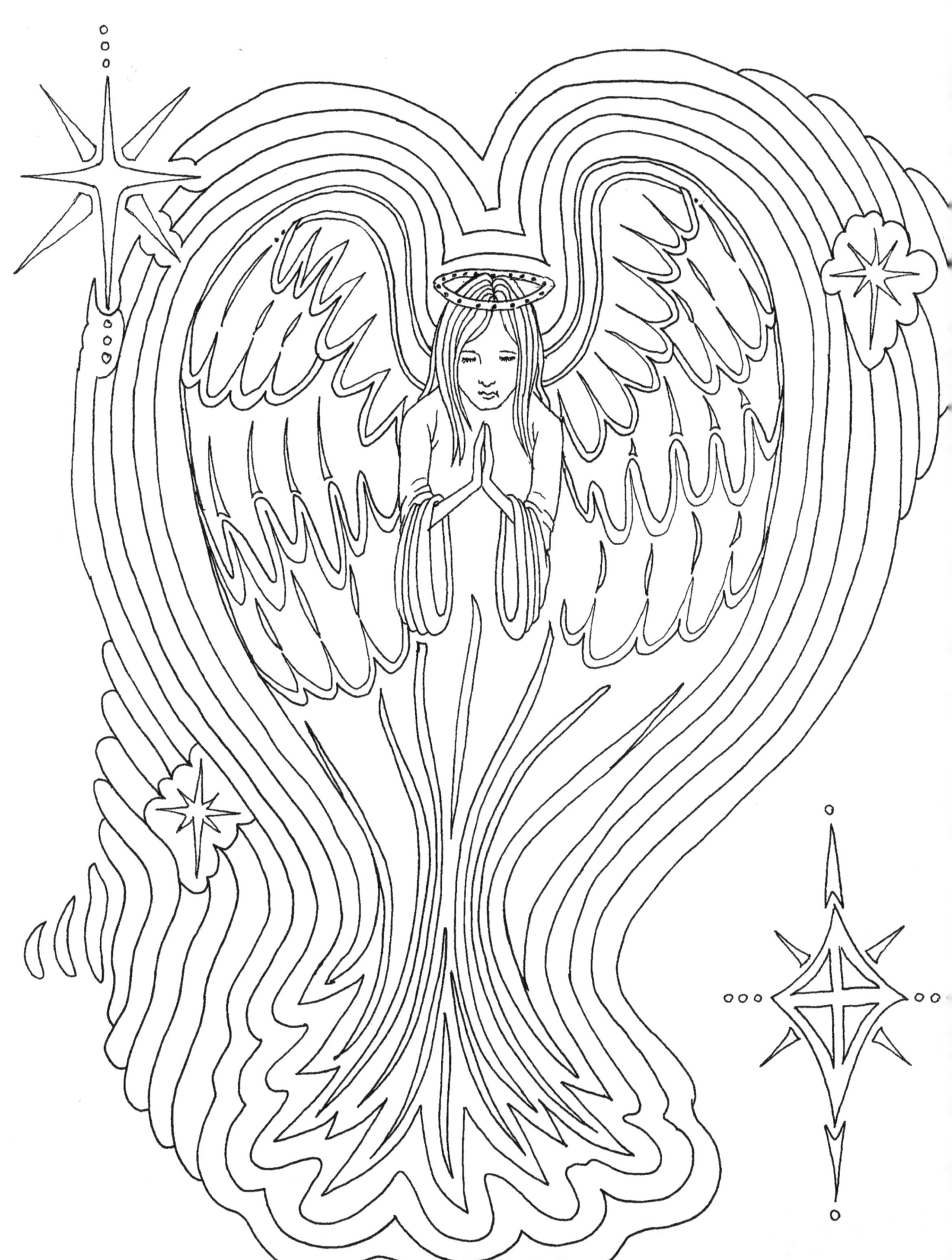

www.ingramcontent.com/pod-product-compliance
Lightning Source LLC
Chambersburg PA
CBHW080646190526
45169CB00009B/3526

ISBN 9781533004833

What Every Member of the Trade Community Should Know About:

Coastwise Trade: Merchandise

AN INFORMED COMPLIANCE PUBLICATION

JANUARY 2009

U.S. CUSTOMS and BORDER PROTECTION